# HOW NOT TO LET ANYBODY BLOCK YOU!

*FROM WHAT IS YOURS.

**THE PERSONAL GUIDE TO BEING PERSISTENT.**

Copyright © 2024 by Brian Ernest Hayward and Published by Brian Hayward for Hayward House Publishing Published by Hayward House and Big Book Box A Member of the Brian Hayward Group All rights reserved. No part of this publication may be reproduced, stored in a retrieval system, or transmitted, in any form or by any means, electronic, mechanical, photocopying, recording, or otherwise, without the prior written permission of the publisher. For information and inquiries , address Hayward House publishing and Hayward Press, Savannah, Ga 31405, Library of Congress Cataloging-in-Publication Data. Hayward, Brian. TITLE=In Jesus Mighty Name Series, Journal WRITING for success in your life / Brian Hayward. p. cm.

PAPERBACK EDITION

## ISBN: 9798333663801
## Imprint:
## Independently published

Self-control. 2. Self-management (Psychology) 3. Success. 4. Success in business. 31405, or visit us at https://www.amazon.com/Brian-Ernest-Hayward/e/B06XT464NM

**PRAYER FOR MYSELF AND MY READERS**

I was taught by my teacher, Pastor Bill Winston, this prayer. This prayer has served me well, and in due time it will serve you well. Father I come before you in Jesus name, thank you for the anointing that's on me and these lips of clay. I know that because of your blessing, I speak this word today with excellency, accuracy, and boldness. I thank you for thinking through my mind and speaking through my lips and this word will come forth unhindered, and unchecked by any outside force. Now I give you the praise for it and I fully expect signs, wonders, and miracles to confirm your word preached in Jesus name,

**AUTHOR BIOGRAPHY**

Brian Ernest Hayward is a passionate Author and Inspirational Speaker, internationally known for his unwavering dedication to creating positive change through the power of words. From religious and success books, to adult coloring books and artist BUSINESS, HOW-TO BOOKS, his writings touch on over 400 different subjects. Today, all of Brian's publications are sold worldwide across multiple formats (Paperback, Kindle, and Large Print) and are translated into 21 different languages. He has also participated in over 100 speaking engagements spanning over 38 states.

# Table Of Contents

Introduction — 7

## Chapter 1: Identifying Potential Blockers — 18

## Chapter 2: Setting Clear Goals — 27

## Chapter 3: Building Confidence and Assertiveness — 34

## Chapter 4: Seeking Supportive Networks — 37

## Chapter 5: Staying Focused and Persistent — 40

## Chapter 6: Developing Problem-Solving Skills — 43

## Chapter 7: Communicating Effectively — 46

## Chapter 8: Setting and Enforcing — 49

## Chapter 9: Adapting and Being Flexible — 64

## Chapter 10: Focusing on Self-Improvement — 74

## Bonus Chapter 1: Harnessing the Power of Positivity — 85

## Bonus Chapter 2: Leveraging Technology for Persistence — 106

Bibliography — 146

NOTES — 147

"How to Not Let Anybody Block You! From What is Yours (A Personal Guide to Being Persistent)"

# Introduction

## "How to Not Let Anybody Block You! From What is Yours (A Personal Guide to Being Persistent)"

Welcome to "How to Not Let Anybody Block You! From What is Yours (A Personal Guide to Being Persistent)." This is not just a book; it is your personal toolkit for  navigating the sometimes-treacherous waters of life and business, ensuring that nothing and no one can stand in your way. Whether climbing the corporate ladder, starting your own venture, or simply trying to get through the day with your sanity intact, this book is here to help you hustle, persevere, and triumph.

Now, let us talk about the journey of authoring this book, which spanned three intense, caffeine-fueled months. In month one, the groundwork was laid. This included extensive research into Persistence's psychological and social dynamics, consultations with 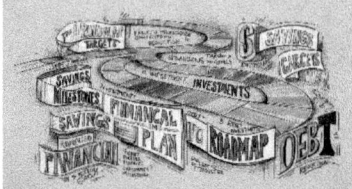 experts in various fields, and plenty of personal anecdotes about facing and overcoming blocks. Month two was all about structure and content creation. Chapters were meticulously outlined, key concepts were expanded upon, and the first drafts began to take speaking on the three; the focus shifted to refining and polishing. Feedback was incorporated, humor was injected (because who does not need a good laugh when tackling severe subjects?), and the final changes were added to create a cohesive, engaging, and practical guide.

So why a book about not letting anyone block you? Because, let us face it, life is full of potential blockers. These can be people, circumstances, or doubts and fears.  This book is not about identifying these blockers and the tools and mindset needed to bulldoze through them. Persistence is the key to unlocking your potential and achieving your goals, and this book will show you how to cultivate and harness that Persistence in a way that is both effective and enjoyable.

In high-stakes businesses, Persistence is often the difference between success and failure. It is not  always the most brilliant or talented who succeed; it is those who refuse to give up. This book provides the strategies to keep pushing forward, no matter your obstacles. We will explore real-world examples and case studies, offering insights from those who have walked the path before you. Their stories of grit and determination will inspire you and provide practical lessons you can apply in your journey.

Persistence is needed in every corner of the world and in every aspect of life. In the fast-paced business environment, you must be persistent and strive to achieve your goals despite setbacks and challenges. It means not letting office politics, market fluctuations, or personal doubts derail your progress. The principles outlined in this book are universally applicable, whether negotiating a big deal, managing a team, or simply trying to get your foot in the door.

One of the critical elements of Persistence is goal-setting—but not just any goals—SMART (Specific, Measurable, Achievable, Relevant, and Time-bound). This book will guide you through setting these goals and creating a roadmap to achieve them. We will break down the importance of having an unobstructed vision, the steps to create a strategy, and the tools you need to stay on track. By the end of this book, you will not only know how to set goals but also how to crush them.

Another cornerstone of Persistence is resilience. Life will throw curveballs at you, and how you respond to them will determine your success. This book delves into building resilience, offering techniques to bounce back from setbacks more robust than before. We will look at the science behind resilience, practical exercises to enhance it, and inspiring stories of people who have overcome incredible odds. You will learn to turn adversity into an advantage and keep moving forward.

Communication is crucial to ensuring you are not blocked from what is rightfully yours. Effective communication is essential, whether negotiating terms, presenting ideas, or standing up for yourself. This book provides tips and techniques for assertive communication. We will cover everything from body language to active listening, ensuring you can express your needs and boundaries clearly and confidently.

A supportive network is invaluable in your persistence journey. No one succeeds in isolation, and a solid support system can make all the difference. This book will teach you how to build and maintain a network of allies who will encourage and assist you. We will cover everything from finding mentors to leveraging social media for professional connections. You will learn the art of networking and how to create mutually beneficial relationships.

Focus and time management are also vital components of Persistence. This book will help you master these skills, offering practical tips to eliminate distractions and prioritize tasks effectively. We will explore techniques like the Pomodoro Technique, time blocking, and the use of productivity apps. By managing your time efficiently, you will be able to maintain momentum and make consistent progress toward your goals.

But what about those moments when you are ready to give up? When everything is going wrong, and you are questioning whether it is all worth it? This book addresses these moments head-on. We will discuss the importance of maintaining a positive mindset, the role of self-care, and how to find motivation even in the darkest times. You will learn strategies to keep your spirits high and your eyes on the prize, no matter how tough things get.

Of course, none of this would be complete without real-life examples and case studies. Throughout the book, you will find stories of individuals who have faced and overcome significant blockers. Their experiences provide valuable lessons and proof that Persistence pays off. These case studies are inspirational and packed with practical advice that you can apply to your own situations. We have sprinkled in plenty of humor.

To ensure this book is informative and humorous persistence is serious business, but that does not mean we cannot have fun along the way. You will find amusing anecdotes, witty observations, and even a few dad jokes to keep you entertained. Learning to be persistent should not be a slog but an enjoyable and enriching experience.

"How to Not Let Anybody Block You! From What is Yours (A Personal Guide to Being Persistent)" is more than just a guide; it is a call to action. It challenges you to take control of your destiny, refuse to be sidelined, and relentlessly pursue what is rightfully yours. Whether you are a seasoned professional or just starting out, the principles in this book will equip you with the tools you need to succeed.

So, buckle up and get ready to dive into a journey of self-discovery, empowerment, and unyielding Persistence. By the time you turn the last page, you will be armed with the knowledge and strategies to ensure  that nothing and no one can block you from achieving your dreams. Let us start this incredible journey together and unlock your full potential.

# Chapter 1: Identifying Potential Blockers

## Recognizing Blockers

Understanding who or what is blocking your path is the first step to overcoming obstacles. Blockers come in two primary flavors: intentional and unintentional. Intentional blockers are those   individuals who actively work to hinder your progress. They might be motivated by jealousy, competition, or plain old malice. Recognizing these blockers involves keen observation and sometimes a bit of detective work. Look for patterns of behavior that suggest sabotage, such as spreading rumors or creating unnecessary roadblocks.

Unintentional blockers, on the other hand, are often well-meaning individuals who inadvertently stand in your way. These can be family members, friends, or colleagues who create obstacles out of a desire to protect or support you. They might advise caution when taking risks or offer unsolicited advice that sows doubt in your mind. While their intentions are usually good, the effect is the same: your progress is hindered.

## Understanding Motivations

Intentional blockers often act out of jealousy and insecurity. They see your success as a threat to their own status or self-worth. Understanding this motivation can help you develop empathy and strategic responses. Instead of confronting them directly, which can escalate the situation, try to address their insecurities indirectly. Show them how your success can benefit them, turning potential adversaries into allies.

Competition is another common motivator. In highly competitive environments, such as the workplace, individuals may resort to blocking tactics to get ahead. Recognizing this behavior requires a nuanced understanding of office dynamics. Pay attention to who seems overly concerned with others' achievements and who frequently downplays or criticizes their colleagues' successes. These are the competitive blockers

**Common Scenarios**

In the workplace, blockers can take many forms. Office politics often play a significant role, with colleagues who may feel threatened by your capabilities trying to undermine you. They might do this by withholding information, giving you less credit than you deserve, or subtly influencing others against you. Understanding these dynamics is crucial to navigating and overcoming them.

Personal relationships also harbor potential blockers. Friends and family members might not always understand or support your goals, mainly if they differ significantly from their own. For instance, pursuing an unconventional career might meet with resistance from parents who prefer a more stable path. Recognizing these well-meaning but obstructive influences is the first step to addressing them.

### Recognizing Blockers

Intentional blockers are easy to spot once you know what to look for. They often exhibit behaviors aimed at undermining your efforts, such as spreading false information, creating unnecessary complications, or directly opposing your initiatives. These actions are typically consistent and patterned, making them identifiable if you pay attention. Keeping a record of such incidents can help you build a case if needed.

Unintentional blockers might require a more nuanced approach. These individuals do not mean to hinder you, but their actions or advice can be more challenging to address because it often involves close relationships. A gentle but firm conversation, where you explain how their actions impact you, can usually resolve these issues without causing friction.

**Understanding Motivations**

   Jealousy and insecurity often drive intentional blockers. They perceive your success as a threat to their own status or achievements. This is common in competitive environments where success is evident and prized. Recognizing this can help you approach the situation with empathy and strategy. Sometimes, showing these individuals how they can benefit from your success can mitigate their obstructive behavior.

   Competition can also drive blocking behavior. In workplaces with limited opportunities for advancement, colleagues might see your progress as a direct threat to their career prospects. Understanding this dynamic can help you navigate these challenges more effectively. Building alliances and finding ways to collaborate can reduce the tension and foster a more supportive environment.

## Common Scenarios

Workplace dynamics often involve a mix of intentional and unintentional blockers. In highly competitive  fields, colleagues might resort to underhanded tactics to get ahead. These can include sabotaging your projects, spreading false rumors, or undermining your credibility. Recognizing these behaviors early can help you take proactive strategies.

In personal relationships, blockers might not always recognize the impact of their actions. Family members might discourage you from pursuing risky ventures out of a desire to protect you, not realizing that they are stifling your ambitions. Friends might project their own fears and insecurities onto you, advising caution when you need to take bold steps. Understanding these dynamics can help you address them constructively.

## Recognizing Blockers

Intentional blockers exhibit consistent patterns of obstructive behavior. They might spread false information, create unnecessary  obstacles, or directly oppose your initiatives. These actions are often motivated by jealousy, competition, or insecurity. Recognizing these patterns involves keen observation and sometimes documenting incidents to identify recurring themes.

Unintentional blockers, on the other hand, might not realize they are standing in your way. These individuals can be more challenging because their intentions are good. They might offer advice that, while well-meaning, sows doubt and caution when you need to be bold and decisive. Addressing these issues requires tact and empathy, often involving honest conversations about how their actions affect Motivations.

Jealousy and insecurity are common motivators for intentional blockers. They perceive your success as a threat to their own status or achievements. This is especially true in competitive environments where visibility and recognition are highly prized. Understanding these motivations can help you develop strategies to mitigate their impact. Showing these individuals how your success can benefit them can turn potential adversaries into allies.

Competition is another significant motivator. In environments where opportunities are scarce, colleagues might resort to blocking tactics to advance their own careers. Recognizing this dynamic involves paying close attention to who frequently downplays others' successes or

engages in subtle undermining behaviors. Building alliances and fostering a collaborative environment can help reduce the sense of competition and create a more supportive atmosphere.

### Common Scenarios

In the workplace, blockers can take many forms. Office politics often play a significant role, with colleagues who feel threatened by your capabilities trying to undermine you. They might do this by withholding crucial information, giving you less credit than you deserve, or subtly influencing others against you. Recognizing these dynamics is essential to navigating and overcoming them.

Personal relationships also harbor potential blockers. Friends and family might not always understand or support your goals, mainly if they differ significantly from their own. For instance, pursuing an unconventional career might meet with resistance from parents who prefer a more stable path. Recognizing these well-meaning but obstructive influences is the first step to addressing them constructively.

## Chapter 2: Setting Clear Goals

### Defining Objectives

The foundation of Persistence lies in setting clear, achievable goals. The SMART framework is an excellent starting point. SMART stands for Specific, Measurable, Achievable, Relevant, and Time-bound. These criteria help ensure that your goals are well-defined and attainable. A specific goal clarifies precisely what you want to achieve, leaving no room for ambiguity. Measurable goals allow you to track your progress and ensure you stay on the right path.

Achievable goals are realistic and consider your current resources and constraints. Setting goals that challenge you but are still within reach is essential. Relevant goals align with your broader objectives and values, ensuring that your efforts are directed toward meaningful outcomes. Finally, time-bound goals have a clear deadline, providing a sense of urgency and helping you stay focused.

**Creating a Roadmap**

Once you have defined your goals, the next step is to create a roadmap to achieve them. This involves breaking down larger objectives into smaller, manageable tasks. This process, known as chunking, makes the overall goal less daunting and helps you progress steadily. Each task should be specific and time-bound, contributing to the larger goal.

Establishing a timeline with key milestones is crucial for tracking progress. Milestones serve as checkpoints, allowing you to assess how far you have come and what needs to be done. This structured approach not only keeps you organized but also gives you a sense of accomplishment as you reach each milestone, boosting your motivation and Persistence.

**Tools and Techniques**

In the digital age, numerous tools and techniques can help you set and track your goals. Goal-setting apps like Trello or Asana offer features like task lists, deadlines, and progress tracking. These apps can synchronize across devices, ensuring you always have your goals and tasks at your fingertips. Utilizing Technology can significantly enhance your ability to stay organized and focused.

Journaling is another powerful technique. Writing down your goals and regularly reflecting on your progress provides valuable insights and motivates you. Your journals can serve as a personal accountability tool, reminding you of your commitments and helping you identify areas for improvement. Combining journaling with digital tools can create a comprehensive system for goal management.

## Defining Objectives

The clarity of your objectives determines the effectiveness of your efforts. Specific goals eliminate ambiguity, allowing you to focus your energy on concrete outcomes. Measurable goals provide benchmarks for tracking progress, ensuring you stay on course. Achievable goals consider resources and constraints, making them realistic and attainable.

Relevant goals align with your broader objectives and values, ensuring that your efforts are directed toward meaningful outcomes. Time-bound goals have clear deadlines, providing a sense of urgency and helping you focus. The SMART framework is an excellent tool for setting well-defined and attainable goals, providing a solid foundation for your persistent efforts.

## Creating a Roadmap

Breaking down larger objectives into smaller, manageable tasks is essential for maintaining momentum. This process, known as chunking, makes the overall goal less daunting and helps you progress steadily. Each task should be specific and time-bound, contributing to the larger goal. Establishing a timeline with key milestones is crucial for tracking progress and maintaining focus.

Milestones serve as checkpoints, allowing you to assess how far you have come and what needs to be done. This structured approach not

It not only keeps you organized but also provides a sense of accomplishment as you reach each milestone. Celebrating these small victories can boost your motivation and Persistence, keeping you on track toward your goal.

### Tools and Techniques

Goal-setting apps like Trello or Asana offer features like task lists, deadlines, and progress tracking. These apps can synchronize across devices, ensuring you always have your goals and tasks at your fingertips. Utilizing Technology can significantly enhance your ability to stay organized and focused. Combining digital tools with traditional methods, like journaling, can create a comprehensive system for goal management.

Journaling allows you to write down your goals and reflect on your progress regularly. This practice can provide valuable insights and keep you motivated. Journals serve as a personal accountability tool, reminding you of your commitments and helping you identify areas for improvement. Integrating journaling with digital tools can enhance your goal-setting process and ensure consistent progress.

## Chapter 3: Building Confidence and Assertiveness

### Developing Self-Confidence

Self-confidence is the cornerstone of persistence. Without it, every obstacle can  seem insurmountable. Positive self-talk is a powerful technique for building self-confidence. By replacing negative thoughts with positive affirmations, you can reinforce your belief in your abilities. Visualization is another effective tool. By imagining yourself succeeding, you can boost your confidence and prepare yourself mentally for challenges.

Confidence is not an innate trait but a skill that can be developed. Start by setting small, achievable goals that allow you to experience success and build momentum. Each success reinforces your belief in your abilities, creating a positive feedback loop. Surrounding yourself with supportive individuals who encourage and believe in you can also significantly enhance your self-confidence.

## Practicing Assertive Communication

Assertive communication is essential for standing your ground and expressing your needs clearly.  Using "I" statements is a crucial technique. Instead of saying, "You never listen to me," say, "I feel unheard when you talk over me." This approach reduces defensiveness and focuses on expressing your feelings and needs. Active listening is equally important. It involves fully engaging with the speaker, understanding their perspective, and responding thoughtfully.

Practicing assertive communication involves setting clear boundaries and being firm yet respectful. It is about expressing your needs and opinions confidently without being aggressive or passive. Assertiveness can help you navigate difficult conversations and ensure your voice is heard, making it a crucial skill for overcoming blockers.

## Real-Life Examples

Studying successful leaders can provide valuable insights into how confidence and assertiveness contribute to overcoming obstacles. Many leaders have faced significant challenges but used their confidence and assertiveness to navigate these difficulties. Reading biographies or listening to interviews can provide practical examples and inspiration.

Personal stories of individuals who have overcome blockers through confidence and assertiveness can also  be motivating. These stories highlight the importance of believing in yourself and standing up for your needs. They provide relatable examples of how Persistence, confidence, and assertiveness can help you overcome even the most challenging obstacles.

## Chapter 4: Seeking Supportive Networks
### Building Positive Relationships

Having a supportive network is crucial for maintaining Persistence.  Identifying allies who genuinely support your goals can encourage and motivate you to keep going. These allies can be friends, family members, or colleagues who share your vision and offer constructive feedback. Building positive relationships involves being open, honest, and supportive in return.

Cultivating mentorships is another effective strategy. Mentors can provide guidance, advice, and support based on their experiences. They can help you navigate challenges, offer different perspectives, and connect you with valuable resources. Finding the right mentor involves identifying individuals whose experiences and values align with your goals.

**Networking Strategies**

Joining professional networks and industry groups can provide valuable opportunities for growth and support. These networks offer a platform to connect with like-minded individuals, share knowledge, and collaborate on projects. Attending industry events, conferences, and seminars can help you expand your network and stay updated on industry trends.

Social media can also be a powerful tool for networking. Platforms like LinkedIn allow you to connect with professionals in your field, join relevant groups, and engage in discussions. Leveraging social media effectively involves being active, sharing valuable content, and building relationships based on mutual interests and respect.

**Maintaining Relationships**

Building a network is the first step; maintaining those relationships is equally important. Regular check-ins with your network can help you stay connected and strengthen your relationships. This can involve sending a quick message, scheduling regular catchups, or simply interesting articles and resources.

Mutual support is the foundation of any strong network. Offering help to others, whether through advice, feedback, or resources, can create a  positive, reciprocal relationship. Being there for your network members in times of need can build trust and loyalty, ensuring you have a reliable support system to fall back on when needed.

# Chapter 5: Staying Focused and Persistent

## Maintaining Focus

In a world full of distractions, maintaining focus is essential for persistence. Eliminating distractions involves creating a dedicated workspace, setting clear boundaries, and using tools like website blockers to stay on task. Time management techniques, such as the Pomodoro Technique or time blocking, can help you prioritize tasks and stay organized.

Prioritizing tasks based on their importance and urgency can ensure you stay focused on what matters most. Creating a daily or weekly plan can help you allocate time effectively and avoid getting overwhelmed. Regularly reviewing and adjusting your plan can keep you on track and ensure your efforts align with your goals.

## Cultivating Persistence

Persistence involves developing resilience and staying motivated through tough times. Building resilience requires a mindset shift, viewing setbacks as opportunities for growth rather than failures. Reflecting on past successes and challenges can help you recognize your strengths and areas for improvement, boosting your confidence and Persistence.

Motivational techniques, such as setting small, achievable goals and rewarding yourself for progress, can help you stay motivated. Surrounding yourself with positive influences, such as supportive friends, family, and mentors, can also help. Regularly reminding yourself of your goals and why they matter can reinforce your commitment and Persistence.

## Case Studies

Historical figures who exhibited exceptional Persistence can provide valuable lessons and inspiration. For example, Thomas Edison, who had failed thousands of times before inventing the lightbulb, demonstrated the power of Persistence. Studying such figures can provide practical examples of how Persistence leads to success.

Modern success stories can also be motivating. Entrepreneurs, athletes, and other individuals who have overcome significant obstacles through persistence can offer valuable insights and inspiration. These stories highlight the importance of staying focused, resilient, and motivated, providing relatable examples of how persistence can lead to success.

# Chapter 6: Developing Problem-Solving Skills
## Identifying Obstacles

Effective problem-solving begins with identifying the root cause of the problem. Root cause analysis involves asking why a problem occurred and  drilling down until the fundamental issue is identified. This process can reveal underlying patterns and issues that must be addressed to prevent future problems.

SWOT analysis (Strengths, Weaknesses, Opportunities, Threats) is another valuable tool for identifying obstacles. This analysis helps you understand your current situation, including internal strengths and weaknesses and external opportunities and threats. By identifying these factors, you can develop strategies to overcome barriers and leverage your strengths.

## Critical Thinking and Creativity

Critical thinking involves analyzing information objectively and making reasoned judgments. This skill is crucial for effective problem-solving. Techniques such as the Six Thinking Hats, which involve looking at a problem from different perspectives, can enhance critical thinking skills.

Creativity is also essential for problem-solving. Brainstorming techniques, such as mind mapping and accessible writing, can help generate multiple solutions to a problem. Encouraging diverse perspectives and thinking freely can lead to innovative solutions. Balancing critical thinking and creativity can help you develop practical, well-rounded solutions.

## Practical Application

Problem-solving frameworks like the PDCA (Plan-Do-Check-Act) cycle provide structured problem-solving approaches. These frameworks guide you through identifying the problem, developing solutions, implementing them, and evaluating their effectiveness. Using these structured approaches can enhance your problem-solving skills and increase your chances of success.

Real-world examples of problem-solving can provide valuable insights and inspiration.  Studying how individuals and organizations overcame significant challenges through effective problem-solving can offer practical lessons. These examples demonstrate the importance of Persistence, creativity, and structured approaches to overcoming obstacles.

# Chapter 7: Communicating Effectively

## Open and Honest Communication

Effective communication is crucial for overcoming blockers. Being transparent and precise in your communication can prevent misunderstandings and ensure your message is understood.

Transparency is also essential for building trust. Being open about your intentions, goals, and progress can foster a supportive and collaborative environment.

Maintaining open and honest communication involves being receptive to feedback and willing to share your thoughts and feelings. This approach can build stronger  relationships and create a positive, supportive network. Practicing active listening, where you fully engage with the speaker and respond thoughtfully, can enhance your communication skills.

## Conflict Resolution

Conflict is inevitable, but effective conflict resolution can prevent it from becoming a blocker. Negotiation techniques, such as finding common ground and focusing on win-win solutions, can help resolve conflicts amicably. Mediation skills, where a neutral third party helps facilitate a resolution, can also be valuable.

Conflict resolution involves understanding the underlying issues and addressing them constructively. This might include setting clear boundaries, addressing misunderstandings, or finding mutually beneficial compromises. Developing these skills can help you navigate conflicts effectively and maintain positive relationships.

## Tools for Effective Communication

Various communication platforms can enhance your ability to communicate effectively. Email, instant messaging, and video conferencing tools can facilitate clear and timely communication. Choosing the right platform for your needs and using it effectively can enhance your communication skills.

Feedback mechanisms, such as regular check-ins and performance reviews, can provide valuable insights and help you improve your communication. Encouraging and using feedback to adjust your communication style can build stronger relationships and ensure your message is understood.

# Chapter 8: Setting and Enforcing

## Importance of Boundaries

Boundaries are crucial for protecting your time, energy, and focus. Without clear boundaries, it is easy for others to infringe on your personal space, time, and mental health. Boundaries help maintain a balance between work and personal life, ensuring you will not be overwhelmed by external demands. They allow you to stay focused on your goals without unnecessary distractions.

Setting boundaries is not about saying no to others; it is about saying yes to yourself. It involves recognizing your limits and respecting them. When you establish clear boundaries, you create a framework within which you can operate effectively and efficiently. This framework helps you allocate your resources—time, energy, and attention—to align priorities.

Boundaries also help protect your mental health. They act as a buffer against stress and burnout by ensuring you do not take on more than you can handle. By establishing that you are willing to tolerate, you can reduce the risk of feeling overwhelmed and maintain a healthier work-life balance. This is particularly important in high-pressure environments where the demands on your time and energy demands can be relentless.

## How to Set Boundaries

Setting boundaries begins with self-must. You must understand your limits and what you need to function at your best. This involves identifying non-negotiables for you, such as time for self-care, uninterrupted work hours, or personal space. Once you are clear on your needs, you can start to set boundaries that protect them.

Communicating Effectively The next step is to be clear and assertive about what you need and why. For example, if you need uninterrupted time to focus on a project, let your colleagues know you will not be available during certain hours. Being upfront about your boundaries helps prevent misunderstandings and ensures that others respect your limits.

Setting boundaries also involves being consistent. Putting a boundary once is not enough; you must enforce it consistently. This means standing firm when others push your limits and reminding them of your boundaries when necessary. Consistency helps reinforce your boundaries and clarifies that you are serious about protecting your time and energy.

**Enforcing Boundaries**

Enforcing boundaries requires confidence and assertiveness. It is not always easy to say no or to stand up for your needs, especially if you are worried about offending others or being seen as problematic. However, enforcing your boundaries is essential for maintaining your well-being and staying focused on your goals. Remember, it is not about being selfish but protecting your ability to function effectively.

One key strategy for enforcing boundaries is to be proactive rather than reactive. This means anticipating situations where your boundaries might be challenged and preparing responses in advance. For example, suppose you know colleagues often interrupt you during work hours. In that case, you can set up a signal to indicate when you are unavailable or establish times for meetings and discussions.

Handling pushback is another crucial aspect of enforcing boundaries. When you set and enforce limits, you might encounter resistance from others who are used to having unrestricted access to your time and energy. It is essential to stand firm and reiterate your boundaries calmly and confidently. Over time, people will learn to respect your limits and adjust their expectations accordingly.

## Importance of Boundaries

Boundaries help focus by minimizing distractions and interruptions. In a world where constant connectivity and instant communication are the norms, it is easy to get pulled in multiple directions simultaneously. You can create a more focused and productive environment by setting boundaries around your work time, personal time, and even your digital life. This helps you stay on track with your goals and avoid getting sidetracked by less important tasks.

Boundaries also protect your relationships. When you set clear boundaries, you create a framework for healthy interactions with others. This involves respecting others' boundaries as well as your own. By being clear about your limits, you can prevent misunderstandings and conflicts, ensuring your relationships remain positive and supportive.

Another critical aspect of boundaries is that they help you prioritize your own well-being. In our fast-paced world, it is putting needs ahead of your own. How is easy it ever easy? Consistently doing so can lead to burnout and resentment. By setting boundaries, you ensure that you take care of yourself first, enabling you to be more present and practical in your interactions with others.

## How to Set Boundaries

Identifying your non-negotiables is a crucial first step in setting boundaries. These are the things that you absolutely need to function at your best. They might include time for exercise, uninterrupted work hours, or regular breaks. Being clear about these non-negotiables helps you set realistic and practical boundaries.

Communicating your boundaries involves being clear and assertive without being aggressive. It is essential to explain why you are setting a boundary and how it helps you. For example, you might say, "I need to focus on this project for the next two hours, so I won't be available for meetings during that time." This approach helps others understand your needs and increases the likelihood that they will respect your boundaries.

Setting boundaries also requires flexibility. While being firm about your limits is essential, it is also important to recognize that situations change and sometimes require adjustments. Being willing to revisit and adjust your boundaries as needed ensures they remain effective and practical. This might involve renegotiating deadlines, adjusting your schedule, or finding new ways to communicate your needs.

## Enforcing Boundaries

Enforcing boundaries can be challenging, mainly if you are used to accommodating others' needs at your own expense. However, it is essential for maintaining your well-being and productivity. One effective strategy is to practice assertive communication. This involves being clear and direct about your needs while respecting others. For example, if someone tries to infringe on your work time, you can say, "I'm currently focused on a project and can't talk right now, but I'd be happy to discuss this later."

Another critical aspect of enforcing boundaries is to remain consistent. Once you have set a boundary, it is essential to stick to it. This consistency reinforces the boundary and clarifies that you protect your time and energy seriously. It also helps others learn to respect your limits, reducing the likelihood of future boundary violations.

Handling pushback requires a calm and confident approach. When others resist your boundaries, standing firm and reiterating your needs is important. This might involve repeating your boundary or explaining why it is essential. Over time, people will come to understand and respect your limits, making it easier to maintain your boundaries eventually.

**Importance of Boundaries**

Boundaries are essential for maintaining a healthy work-life balance. In today's always-on culture, letting work spill over into your personal life is easy. Setting clear boundaries helps ensure that you have time to relax, recharge, and pursue other interests outside of work. This balance is crucial for your overall well-being and can prevent burnout.

Boundaries also help you stay focused on your priorities. When you set limits on what you are willing to take on, you can concentrate on the tasks and goals that matter most. This focused approach increases your productivity and ensures that you make meaningful progress toward your objectives. By avoiding unnecessary distractions, you can achieve more in less time.

Another critical aspect of boundaries is that they help you build healthier relationships. When you are clear about your limits, you create a framework for respectful interactions with others. This reduces the risk of misunderstandings and conflicts, fostering a more positive and supportive environment. Boundaries also ensure you respect others' limits, contributing to more balanced and harmonious relationships.

**How to Set Boundaries**

Understanding your needs is the first step in setting effective boundaries. This involves reflecting on what is important to you and what you need to function at your best. Identifying these needs helps you set limits that protect your time, energy, and mental health. It is essential to be honest with yourself about what you need and to prioritize these needs when setting boundaries.

Communicating your boundaries effectively involves being clear and assertive. It is essential to explain why you are setting a boundary and how it helps you. This approach increases the likelihood that others will understand and respect your limits. For example, you might say, "I need to focus on this project for the next two hours, so I won't be available for meetings during that time." This transparent communication helps prevent misunderstandings and ensures that your boundaries are respected.

Setting boundaries also requires flexibility. While being firm about your limits is essential, it is also important to recognize that situations change and sometimes require adjustments. Being willing to revisit and adjust your boundaries as needed ensures they remain practical and relevant. This might involve renegotiating deadlines, adjusting your schedule, or finding new ways to communicate your needs.

### Enforcing Boundaries

Enforcing boundaries can be challenging, mainly if you are used to accommodating others' needs at your own expense. However, it is essential for maintaining your well-being and productivity. One effective strategy is to practice assertive communication. This involves being clear and direct about your needs while respecting others. For example, if someone tries to infringe on your work time, you can say, "I'm currently focused on a project and can't talk right now, but I'd be happy to discuss this later."

Another critical aspect of enforcing boundaries is to remain consistent. Once you have set a boundary, it is essential to stick to it. This consistency reinforces the boundary and clarifies that you are serious about protecting your time and energy. It also helps others learn to respect your limits, reducing the likelihood of future boundary violations.

Handling pushback requires a calm and confident approach. When others resist your boundaries, standing firm and reiterating your needs is  important. This might involve repeating your boundary or explaining why it is essential. Over time, people will come to understand and respect your limits, making it easier to maintain your Boundaries overall.

# Chapter 9: Adapting and Being Flexible
## Staying Adaptable

Adaptability is a crucial trait for overcoming obstacles and staying persistent. Adapting to new  situations and challenges is crucial for success in a rapidly changing world. This involves being open to innovative ideas, willing to change your approach, and able to pivot when necessary. Staying adaptable helps you navigate unexpected obstacles and find new ways to achieve your goals.

Embracing change is an essential part of adaptability. Instead of seeing change as a threat, view it as an opportunity for growth and learning. This mindset shift can help you stay positive and proactive when facing challenges. Embracing change also involves being flexible in your plans and willing to adjust your strategies as needed. This flexibility allows you to respond effectively to new situations and continue making progress toward your goals.

Flexibility in plans is crucial for staying adaptable. While having an unclouded vision and goals is essential, it is equally important to be willing to adjust your plans as needed. This might involve changing your approach, reevaluating your priorities, or finding new ways to achieve your objectives. Flexibility in your plans ensures that you can navigate unexpected obstacles and continue progressing, even when things do not go as planned.

**Overcoming Unexpected Barriers**

Contingency planning is a crucial strategy for overcoming unexpected barriers. This involves anticipating potential obstacles and developing plans to address them. By preparing for challenges in advance, you can reduce the impact of these obstacles and ensure that you have a clear path forward. Contingency planning helps you stay proactive and prepared, increasing your chances of success.

An agile mindset is also essential for overcoming unexpected barriers. This involves being willing to adapt and change your approach as needed. An agile mindset helps you stay flexible and responsive, allowing you to navigate new challenges effectively. This approach is particularly important in rapidly changing environments where unexpected obstacles can arise at any time.

Examples of adaptability can provide valuable insights and inspiration. Studying how business leaders and successful individuals have navigated unexpected obstacles through adaptability can offer practical lessons. These examples highlight the importance of staying flexible, proactive, and resilient in facing challenges. By learning from others' experiences, you can develop strategies to overcome obstacles and stay on track toward your goals.

**Staying Adaptable**

Adaptability involves being open to innovative ideas and approaches. In a rapidly changing world, being able to adapt to new situations and challenges is crucial for success. This openness helps you stay flexible and responsive, allowing you to navigate unexpected obstacles effectively. Staying adaptable involves being willing to change your approach, reevaluate your priorities, and find new ways to achieve your goals.

Embracing change is an essential part of adaptability. Instead of seeing change as a threat, view it as an opportunity for growth and learning. This mindset shift can help you stay positive and proactive in facing challenges. Embracing change also involves being flexible in your plans and willing to adjust your strategies as needed. This flexibility allows you to respond effectively to new situations and continue making progress toward your goals.

Flexibility in plans is crucial for staying adaptable. While having an unclouded vision and goals is important, it is equally important to be willing to adjust your plans as needed. This might involve changing your approach, reevaluating your priorities, or finding new ways to achieve your objectives. Flexibility in your plans ensures that you can navigate unexpected obstacles and continue progressing, even when things do not go as planned.

### Overcoming Unexpected Barriers

Contingency planning is a crucial strategy for overcoming unexpected barriers. This involves anticipating potential obstacles and developing plans to address them. By preparing for challenges in advance, you can reduce the impact of these obstacles and ensure that you have a clear path forward. Contingency planning helps you stay proactive and prepared, increasing your chances of success.

An agile mindset is also essential for overcoming unexpected barriers. This involves being willing to adapt and change your approach as needed. An agile mindset helps you stay flexible and responsive, allowing you to navigate new challenges effectively. This approach is particularly important in rapidly changing environments where unexpected obstacles can arise at any time.

Examples of adaptability can provide valuable insights and inspiration. Studying how business leaders and successful individuals have navigated unexpected obstacles through adaptability can offer practical lessons. These examples highlight the importance of staying flexible, proactive, and resilient in the face of challenges. By learning from others' experiences, you can develop strategies to overcome your own obstacles and stay on track toward your goals.

**Staying Adaptable**

Adaptability involves being open to current ideas and approaches. In a rapidly changing world, being able to adapt to new situations and challenges is crucial for success. This openness helps you stay flexible and responsive, effectively navigating unexpected obstacles. Staying adaptable involves changing your approach, reevaluating your priorities, and finding new ways to achieve your goals.

Embracing change is an essential part of adaptability. Instead of seeing change as a threat, view it as an opportunity for growth and learning. This mindset shift can help you stay positive and proactive in the face of challenges. Embracing change also involves being flexible in your plans and willing to adjust your strategies as needed. This flexibility allows you to respond effectively to new situations and continue making progress toward your goals.

Flexibility in plans is crucial for staying adaptable. While having a sharp vision and goals is important, it is equally essential to be willing to adjust your plans as needed. This might involve changing your approach, reevaluating your priorities, or finding new ways to achieve your objectives. Being flexible in your plans ensures that you can navigate unexpected obstacles and continue making progress, even when things do not go as planned.

**Overcoming Unexpected Barriers**

Contingency planning is a key strategy for overcoming unexpected barriers. This involves anticipating potential obstacles and developing plans to address them. By preparing for potential challenges in advance, you can reduce the impact of these obstacles and ensure that you have a clear path forward. Contingency planning helps you stay proactive and prepared, increasing your chances of success.

An agile mindset is also essential for overcoming unexpected barriers. This involves being willing to adapt and change your approach as needed. An agile mindset helps you stay flexible and responsive, effectively navigating new challenges. This approach is particularly important in rapidly changing environments where unexpected obstacles can arise at any time.

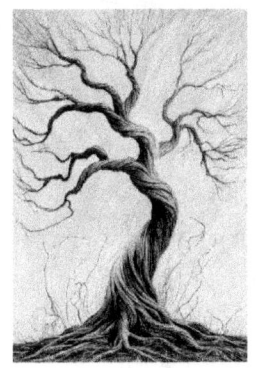

Examples of adaptability can provide valuable insights and inspiration. Studying how business leaders and successful individuals have navigated unexpected obstacles through adaptability can offer practical lessons. These examples highlight the importance of staying flexible, proactive, and resilient in the face of challenges. By learning from others' experiences, you can develop strategies to overcome obstacles and stay on track toward your goals.

# Chapter 10: Focusing on Self-Improvement
## Continuous Learning

Continuous learning is the cornerstone of self-improvement. In a rapidly changing world, staying updated with new knowledge and skills is crucial for personal and professional growth. This involves seeking educational opportunities, such as courses, workshops, and seminars, to enhance your skills and broaden your understanding. Continuous learning helps you stay relevant and competitive in your field.

Educational opportunities are abundant, and taking advantage of them can significantly enhance your skills and knowledge. This might involve enrolling in online courses, attending workshops, or pursuing advanced degrees. By continually seeking new learning opportunities, you can stay ahead of industry trends and ensure you have the skills needed to succeed.

 Professional development is another key aspect of continuous learning. It involves investing in courses and certifications that enhance your skills and knowledge in your field. Professional development helps you stay competitive and ensures you have the expertise needed to excel in your career. It also provides opportunities to network with other professionals and stay updated on industry trends.

**Personal Growth**

Self-reflection is an essential part of personal growth. Regularly assessing your strengths and weaknesses can help you identify areas for improvement and develop strategies to enhance your skills. This might involve seeking feedback from others, engaging in reflective practices like journaling, or taking time to reflect on your experiences. Self-reflection helps you stay aware of your progress and adjust as needed.

Goal revision is another crucial aspect of personal growth. As you learn and grow, your goals may change. Regularly revisiting and revising your goals ensures they align with your evolving priorities and values. This process helps you focus on what matters most and ensures that your efforts are directed toward meaningful outcomes.

Staying competitive involves keeping up with industry trends and continually seeking ways to innovate  and improve. This might include staying updated on the latest developments in your field, networking with other professionals, or pursuing new opportunities for growth and development. Staying competitive ensures you remain relevant and valuable in your industry, increasing your chances of success.

## Continuous Learning

Educational opportunities are abundant, and taking advantage of them can significantly enhance your skills and knowledge. This might involve enrolling in online courses, attending workshops, or pursuing advanced degrees. By continually seeking new learning opportunities, you can stay ahead of industry trends and ensure you have the skills needed to succeed.

Professional development is another critical, especially continuous learning. This involves investing in courses and certifications that enhance your skills and knowledge in your field. Professional development helps you stay competitive and ensures you have the expertise needed to excel in your career. It also provides opportunities to network with other professionals and stay updated on industry trends.

**Personal Growth**

Self-reflection is an essential part of personal growth. Regularly assessing your strengths and weaknesses can help you identify areas for improvement and develop strategies to enhance your skills. This might involve seeking feedback from others, engaging in reflective practices like journaling, or taking time to reflect on your experiences. Self-reflection helps you stay aware of your progress and adjust as needed.

Goal revision is another crucial aspect of personal growth. As you learn and grow, your goals may change. Regularly revisiting and revising your goals ensures they align with your evolving priorities and values. This process helps you stay focused on what matters most and ensures that.

Your efforts are directed toward meaningful outcomes.

Staying competitive involves keeping up with industry trends and continually seeking ways to innovate and improve. This might include staying updated on the latest developments in your field, networking with other professionals, or pursuing new opportunities for growth and development. Staying competitive ensures you remain relevant and valuable in your industry, increasing your chances of success.

**Continuous Learning**

Educational opportunities are abundant, and taking advantage of them can significantly enhance your skills and knowledge. This might involve enrolling in online courses, attending workshops, or pursuing advanced degrees. By continually seeking learning opportunities, you can stay ahead of industry trends and ensure you have the skills needed to succeed.

Professional development is another key aspect of crucial learning. It involves investing in courses and certifications that enhance your skills and knowledge in your field. Professional development helps you stay competitive and ensures you have the expertise needed to excel in your career. It also provides opportunities to network with other professionals and stay updated on industry trends.

## Personal Growth

Self-reflection is an essential part of personal growth. Regularly assessing your strengths and weaknesses can help you identify areas for improvement and develop strategies to enhance your skills. This might involve seeking feedback from others, engaging in introspective practices like journaling, or taking time to reflect on your experiences. Self-reflection helps you stay aware of your progress and adjust as needed.

Goal revision is another crucial aspect of personal growth. As you learn and grow, your goals may change. Regularly revisiting and revising your goals ensures they align with your evolving priorities and values. This process helps you focus on what matters most and ensures that your efforts are directed toward meaningful outcomes.

Staying competitive involves keeping up with industry trends and continually seeking ways to innovate and improve. This might include staying updated on the latest developments in your field, networking with other professionals, or pursuing new opportunities for growth and development. Staying competitive ensures you remain relevant and valuable in your industry, increasing your chances of success.

**Continuous Learning**

Educational opportunities are abundant, and taking advantage of them can significantly enhance your skills and knowledge. This might involve enrolling in online courses, attending workshops, or pursuing advanced degrees. By continually seeking learning opportunities, you can stay ahead of industry trends and ensure you have the skills needed to succeed.

Professional development is another crucial aspect of continuous learning. This involves investing in courses and certifications that enhance your skills and knowledge in your field. Professional development helps you stay competitive and ensures you have the expertise needed to excel in your career. It also provides opportunities to network with other professionals and stay updated on industry trends.

**Personal Growth**

Self-reflection is an essential part of personal growth. Regularly assessing your strengths and weaknesses can help you identify areas for improvement and develop strategies to enhance your skills. This might involve seeking feedback from others, engaging in reflective practices like journaling, or taking time to reflect on your experiences. Self-reflection helps you stay aware of your progress and adjust as needed.

Goal revision is another crucial aspect of personal growth. As you learn and grow, your goals may change. Regularly revisiting and revising your goals ensures they align with your evolving priorities and values. This process helps you focus on what matters most and ensures that your efforts are directed toward meaningful outcomes.

Staying competitive involves keeping up with industry trends and continually seeking ways to innovate and improve. This might include staying updated on the latest developments in your field, networking with other professionals, or pursuing new opportunities for growth and development. Staying competitive ensures you remain relevant and valuable in your industry, increasing your chances of success.

# Bonus Chapter 1: Harnessing the Power of Positivity

## Embracing a Positive Mindset

Positivity is a powerful tool in the journey of Persistence. A positive mindset boosts your morale and enhances your resilience against obstacles. When you face challenges with a positive outlook, you are more likely to find solutions and maintain your drive. This mindset shift involves focusing on what you can control and looking for the positive aspect in every situation.

Positive thinking can be cultivated through daily practices. Start your day with affirmations that reinforce your goals and self-worth. Statements like, "I am capable of achieving my goals," can set a positive tone for your day. This practice helps counteract negative thoughts that may arise and keeps you focused on your objectives.

## The Role of Gratitude

Gratitude is another powerful component of a positive mindset. By acknowledging and appreciating the good things in your life, you can shift focus from obstacles to challenges. Keeping a gratitude journal, where you write down things you are thankful for daily, can help reinforce this practice. This shift can improve your overall outlook and increase your Persistence.

Expressing gratitude to others also strengthens your positive mindset. Acknowledging the support and kindness of those around you fosters positive relationships and a supportive network. This network can be invaluable when you encounter blocks, as it provides encouragement and assistance.

**Overcoming Negative Influences**

In your journey to maintain positivity, it is crucial to identify and minimize negative influences. These can come from external sources, like negative people or toxic environments, and internal sources, such as self-doubt and fear. Recognizing these influences allows you to address them proactively and protect your positive mindset.

One effective strategy is to limit your exposure to negativity. This might involve reducing time spent with negative individuals or avoiding environments that drain your energy. Instead, seek out positive influences that uplift and inspire you. Surrounding yourself with positivity can help reinforce your own positive mindset.

**Building a Supportive Environment**

Creating a supportive environment is essential for maintaining positivity. This involves cultivating relationships with people who encourage and support your goals. Seek mentors, friends, and colleagues who share your values and are invested in your success. These relationships provide a foundation of support that can help you stay positive and persistent.

Your physical environment also plays a role in supporting positivity. Ensure that your workspace is conducive to focus and productivity. This might involve decluttering, adding inspirational quotes, or creating a comfortable and inviting space. A positive physical environment can enhance your mood and keep you motivated.

**The Power of Positive Language**

The language you use, both in your thoughts and your communication, significantly impacts your mindset. Positive language reinforces positive thinking and helps you maintain a constructive outlook. This involves replacing negative or limiting words with positive and empowering ones. For example, instead of saying, "I can't do this," say, "I am working on finding a solution."

Using positive language in your interactions fosters a supportive and encouraging environment. Complimenting others, expressing gratitude, and offering encouragement all create a positive atmosphere. This positivity not only has a ripple effect on you and gives you positive energy.

**Visualizing Success**

Visualization is a powerful technique for maintaining a positive mindset. By imagining yourself achieving your goals, you reinforce your belief in your abilities and keep your focus on success. Visualization involves creating a detailed mental picture of your desired outcome, including the steps needed to achieve it. This practice can boost your motivation and persistence.

Persistent visualization in your daily routine. Spend a few minutes each day picturing yourself  succeeding in your goals. Imagine the steps you will take, the challenges you will overcome, and the feeling of accomplishment you will experience. This practice keeps your goals at the forefront of your mind and reinforces your positive mindset.

## Affirmations and Mantras

Affirmations and mantras are powerful tools for maintaining positivity. You repeat These positive statements regularly to reinforce your goals and self-belief. Affirmations can address specific goals or general aspects of your mindset, such as confidence and resilience. Repeating these statements daily helps internalize them and strengthens your positive outlook.

Mantras, often shorter and more focused, can be used in moments of stress or challenge. They provide a quick way to center yourself and refocus. For example, a mantra like "I am strong and capable" can be repeated during challenging times to boost confidence and Persistence.

**Positive Habits and Routines**

Developing positive habits and routines supports your overall mindset and persistence. Habits such as regular exercise, healthy eating, and adequate sleep contribute to your physical and mental well-being. These habits provide a sturdy foundation for maintaining a positive outlook and the energy needed to pursue your goals.

Incorporate positive routines into your daily life. This might include a morning routine that sets a positive tone for your day, regular breaks to recharge, and an evening routine that helps you unwind. Consistent positive routines reinforce your mindset and support your Persistence in learning from positive role models.

Role models can provide powerful inspiration and guidance on your journey. Identify individuals who embody the positivity and Persistence you aspire to. These might be public figures, mentors, or friends and family members. Studying their behaviors and attitudes can provide valuable insights into maintaining a positive mindset.

Role models can also provide practical strategies for overcoming challenges. You can learn original approaches and techniques from them for navigating obstacles and maintaining focus. Your success stories can inspire you to stay positive and persistent in facing your own challenges.

**Celebrating Small Wins**

Celebrating small wins is an essential practice for maintaining positivity. Recognizing and celebrating your progress, no matter how small, reinforces your motivation and Persistence. These celebrations provide a sense of accomplishment and help keep You Focused on the positive aspects of your journey.

Make a habit of acknowledging your achievements. This might involve keeping a journal where you note your successes, treating yourself to a small reward, or simply reflecting on your progress. Celebrating small wins keeps you motivated and reinforces your positive mindset.

## Developing Emotional Resilience

Emotional resilience is the ability to bounce back from setbacks and maintain a positive outlook. Developing this resilience involves managing your emotions effectively and maintaining perspective. Techniques such as mindfulness, meditation, and deep breathing can help you stay centered and calm in the face of challenges.

Practicing emotional resilience also involves reframing negative experiences. Instead of viewing setbacks as failures, see them as opportunities for growth and learning. This perspective shift helps you maintain a positive outlook and stay motivated to pursue your goals.

## The Impact of Positive Relationships

Positive relationships play a crucial role in maintaining your mindset and Persistence. Surrounding yourself with supportive and encouraging individuals can boost your motivation and resilience. These relationships provide a network of support that can help you navigate challenges and stay focused on your goals.

Nurture positive relationships by investing time and energy into them. Show appreciation for the support you receive and offer your own support in return. Building strong, positive connections creates a supportive environment that enhances your Persistence and positivity.

## The Role of Self-Compassion

Self-compassion is an essential aspect of maintaining a positive mindset. This involves being kind to yourself, especially during challenging times. Instead of being self-critical, practice self-compassion by acknowledging your efforts and treating yourself with the kindness you would offer a friend.

Self-compassion helps you maintain a positive outlook and resilience. It reduces the impact of setbacks and keeps you motivated to pursue your goals. By practicing self-compassion, you can maintain a healthier and more positive relationship with yourself.

## Positive Self-Talk

Positive self-talk involves replacing negative thoughts with positive affirmations. This practice helps counteract self-doubt and reinforces one's belief in one's abilities. By regularly engaging in positive self-talk, one can maintain a constructive and empowering mindset.

Incorporate positive self-talk into your daily routine. Start your day with affirmations that reinforce your goals and self-worth. Throughout the day, be mindful of your internal dialogue and replace negative thoughts with positive ones. This practice helps maintain your positivity and Persistence.

**Maintaining a Growth Mindset**

A growth mindset involves believing that one's abilities and intelligence can be developed through effort and learning. This mindset contrasts with a fixed mindset, which views abilities as static and unchangeable. Maintaining a growth mindset helps one stay positive and persistent when facing challenges.

Adopt a growth mindset by viewing challenges as opportunities for growth and learning. Embrace the improvement process and focus on your effort rather than the outcome. This perspective shift can enhance your resilience and motivate you to pursue your goals.

**The Benefits of Optimism**

Optimism involves expecting positive outcomes and focusing on the potential for success. This mindset helps you stay motivated and persistent, even when faced with challenges. Optimistic individuals are more likely to take proactive steps to achieve their goals and maintain their drive.

Cultivate optimism by focusing on the positive aspects of your journey and visualizing successful outcomes. Practice gratitude and positive self-talk to reinforce your optimistic outlook. By maintaining an optimistic mindset, you can enhance your Persistence and resilience.

## The Influence of Positivity on Persistence

Positivity and Persistence are intricately linked. A positive mindset enhances resilience and motivation, making it easier to stay focused on your goals. By maintaining positivity, you can overcome obstacles more effectively and sustain your drive over the long term.

Practice positivity through daily habits and routines that reinforce your mindset. Surround yourself with positive influences and engage in activities that uplift and inspire you. By consistently cultivating positivity, you can enhance your Persistence and achieve your goals.

## The Role of Humor

Humor is a powerful tool for maintaining a positive mindset. It helps you stay light-hearted and reduces stress, making it easier to navigate challenges. Incorporating humor into your daily life can boost your mood and motivate you.

Find ways to incorporate humor into your routine. This might involve watching a funny video, sharing jokes with friends, or finding the humor in everyday situations. Humor helps you maintain perspective and stay positive, enhancing your persistence.

Positive visualization involves imagining yourself successfully achieving your goals. This practice reinforces your belief in your abilities and keeps you focused on success. Visualization techniques can boost your motivation and Persistence.

Incorporate positive visualization into your daily routine. Spend a few minutes each day picturing yourself succeeding in your goals. Imagine the steps you will take, the challenges you will overcome, and the feeling of accomplishment you will experience. This practice keeps your goals at the forefront of your mind and reinforces your positive mindset.

## The Power of Positive Goals

Setting positive goals involves framing your objectives in a positive light. Instead of focusing on what you want to avoid, focus on what you want to achieve. This positive framing enhances your motivation and persistence.

Reframe your goals to focus on positive outcomes. For example, instead of saying, "I want to stop procrastinating," say, "I want to use my time effectively to achieve my goals." This positive focus keeps you motivated and reinforces your commitment to your objectives.

### Maintaining Long-Term Positivity

Maintaining long-term positivity requires consistent effort and commitment. This involves regularly engaging in practices that reinforce your positive mindset and help you stay focused on your goals. Long-term positivity enhances Persistence and resilience.

Develop a plan for maintaining positivity over the long term. This might involve setting regular check-ins to assess your mindset, seeking new sources of inspiration, and staying connected with your support network. By consistently cultivating positivity, you can sustain your Persistence and achieve your goals.

# Bonus Chapter 2: Leveraging Technology for Persistence

## The Role of Technology in Persistence

In today's digital age, Technology plays a significant role in supporting Persistence in today's digital age. From productivity apps to online learning platforms, Technology offers numerous tools to enhance your ability to stay focused and motivated. Leveraging these tools effectively can help you overcome obstacles and achieve your goals.

Technology provides access to a wealth of resources and information. This can help you stay informed and updated on the latest developments in your field. You can find novel solutions and strategies to overcome challenges by staying connected to a broader knowledge network.

**Productivity Apps and Tools**

Productivity apps are essential tools for maintaining focus and managing your time effectively. Apps like "[Trello](.)", "[Asana](.)", and "[Todoist](.)" help you organize tasks, set deadlines, and track progress. These tools can enhance your ability to stay on top of your goals and avoid getting overwhelmed.

Choose productivity apps that align with your needs and preferences. Some apps offer simple to-do lists, while others provide more complex project management features. Experiment with different tools to find the best work for you and integrate them into your daily routine.

### Time Management Techniques

Technology can enhance your time management skills through various techniques and tools. Calendar apps like Google Calendar and Outlook help you schedule your tasks and allocate your time effectively. These apps provide reminders and notifications to keep you on track and ensure that you meet your deadlines.

Incorporate time management techniques into your routine. This might involve using the Pomodoro Technique, where you work in focused intervals with regular breaks, or time blocking, where you allocate specific blocks of time for different tasks. These techniques can help you stay focused and productive throughout the day.

### Online Learning Platforms

Online learning platforms like Coursera, Udemy, and LinkedIn Learning provide access to various courses and educational resources. These platforms offer opportunities to enhance your skills and knowledge, keeping you competitive and informed. Leveraging these resources can support your Persistence by providing new insights and strategies.

Explore online courses that align with your goals and interests. These courses can help you stay updated on the latest trends in your field and provide practical skills that enhance your ability to overcome challenges. By continuously learning and growing, you can maintain your Persistence and achieve your objectives.

### Networking and Collaboration Tools

Networking and collaboration tools like LinkedIn, Slack, and Microsoft Teams help you connect with others and build supportive relationships. These tools facilitate communication and collaboration, allowing you to share ideas, seek feedback, and find support. Building a solid network can enhance your Persistence by providing encouragement and resources.

Engage with your professional network regularly. Participate in online discussions, attend virtual events, and collaborate on projects. These interactions help you stay connected and informed, providing valuable insights and support. Leveraging networking and collaboration tools can strengthen your Persistence and help you achieve your goals.

## Health and Wellness Apps

Health and wellness apps, such as MyFitnessPal, Headspace, and Calm, support overall well-being. These apps provide tools for tracking physical activity, managing diet, and practicing mindfulness. Maintaining health and well-being is crucial for sustaining Persistence and motivation.

Incorporate health and wellness practices into your daily routine. Use fitness apps to set exercise goals, meditation apps to manage stress, and nutrition apps to maintain a healthy diet. By prioritizing your well-being, you can enhance your energy levels and resilience, supporting your Persistence in achieving your goals.

## Financial Management Tools

Monetary management tools, such as Mint, YNAB (You Need a Budget), and QuickBooks, help you manage your finances effectively. These tools provide insights into your spending, savings, and investments, helping you stay on top of your financial goals. Financial stability can reduce stress and enhance your ability to focus on your objectives.

Use fiscal management tools to create and track your budget, monitor expenses, and plan for future goals. By managing your finances effectively, you can reduce financial stress and allocate more resources toward achieving your personal and professional goals. Financial stability supports your Persistence and overall well-being.

### Goal setting and Tracking Apps

Goal setting and tracking apps, such as OnTrack, Strides, and Habitica, help you set, monitor, and achieve your goals. These apps provide features for setting specific, measurable, achievable, relevant, and time-bound (SMART) goals, tracking progress, and celebrating achievements. Using these tools can enhance your Persistence.

Set clear and achievable goals using goal-setting apps. Break down your larger goals into smaller, manageable tasks and track your progress regularly. Celebrate your achievements along the way to stay motivated and focused. These tools can help you stay organized and persistent in pursuing your objectives.

## Communication Tools

Effective communication is essential for maintaining Persistence. Communication tools, such as Zoom, Skype, and WhatsApp, facilitate clear and timely communication with others. These tools help you stay connected with your network, seek support, and collaborate on projects. Persuasive communication enhances your ability to overcome challenges and achieve your goals.

Use communication tools to stay in touch with your support network. Schedule regular check-ins, virtual meetings, and collaborative sessions to maintain strong relationships. Effective communication gives you the support and resources to stay persistent and focused on your goals.

**Technology for Motivation**

Technology can also enhance your motivation through various apps and tools. Motivation apps, such as Forest, HabitBull, and Fabulous, provide features that encourage positive habits, track your progress, and offer reward tools to boost your motivation and help you stay committed to your goals.

Incorporate motivation apps into your routine. Use them to set daily goals, track your habits, and celebrate your progress. These tools provide reminders and encouragement to keep you focused and motivated. Leveraging Technology for motivation can enhance your Persistence and help you achieve your objectives.

## The Impact of Social Media

Social media can be a powerful tool for maintaining Persistence. Platforms like Twitter, Instagram, and Facebook offer opportunities to connect with others, share your progress, and find inspiration. Engaging with supportive online communities can provide encouragement and motivation.

Use social media mindfully to enhance your Persistence. Follow accounts that inspire and motivate you, participate in online communities that share your interests, and share your progress to seek support and feedback. By leveraging social media positively, you can stay motivated and connected.

### Digital Planning Tools

Digital planning tools like Evernote, OneNote, and Notion help you organize your tasks, set goals, and track your progress. These tools provide features for creating to-do lists, setting reminders, and storing essential information. Using digital planning tools can enhance your organization and productivity.

Integrate digital planning tools into your routine. Use them to plan your day, set goals, and track your progress. These tools help you stay organized and focused, reducing the risk of feeling overwhelmed. Effective planning enhances your Persistence and enables you to achieve your goals.

## Online Support Groups

Online support groups provide a platform for connecting with others with similar goals and challenges. These groups offer opportunities for sharing experiences, seeking advice, and finding encouragement. Engaging with online support groups can enhance your Persistence by providing a sense of community and support.

Join online support groups that align with your goals and interests. Participate actively by sharing your experiences, offering support to others, and seeking advice when needed. These interactions provide valuable insights and encouragement, strengthening your Persistence.

**Technology for Creativity**

Technology also offers tools for enhancing creativity, which can support your Persistence in finding innovative solutions to challenges. Creative tools like Adobe Creative Cloud, Canva, and Procreate provide platforms for graphic design, digital art, and creative projects. Leveraging these tools can boost your creativity and problem-solving skills.

Explore creative tools that align with your interests and goals. Use them to brainstorm ideas, create visual representations of your goals, and find innovative approaches to challenges. Enhancing your creativity through Technology can support your Persistence and help you achieve your objectives.

## The Role of Technology in Learning from Others

Technology provides access to a wealth of information and resources for learning from others. Podcasts, webinars, and online forums offer opportunities to gain insights from experts and peers. Leveraging these resources can provide valuable knowledge and strategies for overcoming challenges.

Engage with online learning resources regularly. Listen to podcasts, attend webinars, and participate in online discussions to stay informed and inspired. These interactions provide new perspectives and ideas that can enhance your Persistence and help you achieve your goals.

## Technology for Stress Management

Stress management is crucial for maintaining Persistence. Technology offers various tools for managing stress.

Such as meditation apps, relaxation music, and guided breathing exercises. These tools can help you stay calm and focused on the face of challenges.

Incorporate stress management tools into your routine. Use meditation apps like Headspace or Calm to practice mindfulness, listen to relaxation music to unwind, and use guided breathing exercises to manage stress. These practices enhance your resilience and support your Persistence.

### Virtual Mentorship

Virtual mentorship provides opportunities to connect with mentors online. Platforms like LinkedIn and MentorCruise offer tools for finding and connecting with mentors in your field. Engaging with virtual mentors can provide guidance, support, and valuable insights for achieving your goals.

Seek out virtual mentorship opportunities that align with your goals. Connect with mentors with the needed experience and knowledge and engage in regular conversations to seek advice and support. Virtual mentorship enhances your Persistence by providing valuable guidance and encouragement.

## Technology for Tracking Progress

Tracking your progress is essential for maintaining Persistence. Persistence Technology offers various tools for monitoring your goals, habits, and achievements. Apps like Strides, Habitica, and Streaks provide features for setting goals, monitoring progress, and celebrating successes.

Use progress-tracking apps to stay on top of your goals. Set clear and measurable objectives, track your daily habits, and review your progress regularly. Celebrating your achievements along the way keeps you motivated and focused. Leveraging Technology to track progress enhances your Persistence and helps you achieve your objectives.

## The Benefits of Digital Detox

While Technology offers numerous benefits, it is also essential to recognize the value of digital detox. Regular breaks from Technology can help you recharge and maintain a healthy balance. Digital detox involves disconnecting from digital devices to focus on offline activities and personal well-being.

Schedule regular digital detox periods into your routine. Use this time to engage in activities that recharge you, such as spending time in nature, reading, or pursuing hobbies. Digital detox helps you maintain a healthy relationship with Technology and supports your overall well-being and Persistence.

## The Future of Technology and Persistence

The future of Technology holds exciting possibilities for enhancing Persistence. Advances in artificial intelligence, virtual reality, and wearable Technology offer new tools and resources for staying motivated and achieving goals. Embracing these innovations can provide new ways to overcome challenges and stay focused.

Stay informed about emerging technologies and consider how they can support your Persistence. Explore new tools and resources that align with your goals and interests. By leveraging the latest technological advancements, you can enhance your ability to stay persistent and achieve your objectives.

## Integrating Technology with Personal Practices

Integrating Technology with your personal practices can create a comprehensive system for maintaining Persistence. Combining digital tools with traditional methods, such as journaling, goal setting, and mindfulness, provides a balanced approach. This integration enhances one's ability to stay focused and motivated.

Develop a personalized system that integrates Technology with your personal practices. Use digital tools for tracking and organization while maintaining offline practices for reflection and mindfulness. This balanced approach supports Persistence and helps you achieve your goals.

## Technology for Accountability

Accountability is crucial for maintaining persistence, and technology offers various tools for enhancing accountability. Apps like Accountability Buddy, Coach.me, and Beeminder provide features for setting goals, tracking progress, and holding yourself accountable. These tools can enhance your commitment to achieving your objectives.

Use accountability apps to set clear goals and track your progress. Share your goals with others and seek support and feedback from your accountability partners. Leveraging Technology for accountability ensures you stay on track and committed to your goals.

### The Role of Technology in Celebrating Success

Celebrating your successes is essential for maintaining motivation and Persistence. Technology offers tools for tracking and celebrating your achievements, such as milestone-tracking apps and virtual celebration platforms. Using these tools helps you acknowledge your progress and stay motivated.

Incorporate celebration tools into your routine. Use milestone-tracking apps to monitor your progress and plan virtual celebrations to acknowledge your achievements. Celebrating your successes motivates you and reinforces your Persistence in pursuing your goals.

## Technology and the Power of Reflection

Reflection is a powerful practice for maintaining Persistence, and Technology offers tools for enhancing reflection. Apps like Reflectly, Daylio, and Journey provide platforms for journaling and self-reflection. These tools help you gain insights into your progress and adjust as needed.

Use reflection apps to regularly assess your goals, challenges, and achievements. Take time to reflect on your experiences and identify areas for improvement. Leveraging Technology for reflection enhances your self-awareness and supports your Persistence in achieving your objectives.

## Embracing a Balanced Approach

While Technology offers numerous benefits, embracing a balanced approach is essential. Digital tools with offline practices create a comprehensive system for maintaining Persistence. This balance ensures that you leverage the advantages of Technology while prioritizing your well-being and personal growth.

Develop a balanced approach to using Technology. Integrate digital tools for tracking, organization, and learning while maintaining offline practices for reflection, mindfulness, and personal connections. This comprehensive approach enhances your Persistence and helps you achieve your goals.

**THIS CONCLUDES
"How to Not Let Anybody Block
You! From What Is Yours (A
Personal Guide to Being
Persistent)"**

# HOW NOT TO LET ANYBODY BLOCK YOU!

### FROM WHAT IS YOURS.

#### THE PERSONAL GUIDE TO BEING PERSISTENT.

Check Out A Book Bundle From
Brian's Other Famous Titles
"How To Get Past The Gatekeepers and
Get To Your Goal In Life:
A Personal Guide to Being Persistent"

## *Bibliography*

1. **Covey, Stephen R.** *The 7 Habits of Highly Effective People: Powerful Lessons in Personal Change*. Simon & Schuster, 1989.

2. **Hill, Napoleon.** *Think and Grow Rich*. The Ralston Society, 1937.

3. **Kiyosaki, Robert T.** *Rich Dad Poor Dad: What the Rich Teach Their Kids About Money That the Poor and Middle Class Do Not!*. Plata Publishing, 1997.

4. **Tracy, Brian.** *Goals!: How to Get Everything You Want Faster Than You Ever Thought Possible*. Berrett-Koehler Publishers, 2003.

5. **Sinek, Simon.** *Start with Why: How Great Leaders Inspire Everyone to Take Action*. Portfolio, 2009.

6. **Dweck, Carol S.** *Mindset: The New Psychology of Success*. Ballantine Books, 2006.

7. **Vaynerchuk, Gary.** *Crush It!: Why NOW Is the Time to Cash In on Your Passion*. HarperStudio, 2009.

8. **Cardone, Grant.** *The 10X Rule: The Only Difference Between Success and Failure*. Wiley, 2011.

9. **Ferriss, Timothy.** *The 4-Hour Workweek: Escape 9-5, Live Anywhere, and Join the New Rich*. Crown Publishing Group, 2007.

10. **Thiel, Peter.** *Zero to One: Notes on Startups, or How to Build the Future*. Crown Business, 2014.

11. **Collins, Jim.** *Good to Great: Why Some Companies Make the Leap... and Others Don't*. HarperBusiness, 2001.

12. **Schultz, Howard, and Joanne Gordon.** *Onward: How Starbucks Fought for Its Life without Losing Its Soul*. Rodale Books, 2011.

13. **Maxwell, John C.** *The 21 Irrefutable Laws of Leadership: Follow Them and People Will Follow You*. Thomas Nelson, 1998.

14. **Sincero, Jen.** *You Are a Badass at Making Money: Master the Mindset of Wealth*. Viking, 2017.

15. **Dalio, Ray.** *Principles: Life and Work*. Simon & Schuster, 2017.

# NOTES

www.ingramcontent.com/pod-product-compliance
Lightning Source LLC
Chambersburg PA
CBHW071927210526
45479CB00002B/586